WOOD PELLET SMOKER AND GRILL COOKBOOK

The ultimate guide to a perfect barbecue in your homestead or backyard.

Poultry, game, fish and other seafood, vegetable and sauce recipes!

Earl Williams

ISBN: 978-1-80186-105-2

This eBook is provided with the sole purpose of providing relevant information on a specific topic for which every reasonable effort has been made to ensure that it is both accurate and reasonable. Nevertheless, by purchasing this eBook you consent to the fact that the author, as well as the publisher, are in no way experts on the topics contained herein, regardless of any claims as such that may be made within.

As such, any suggestions or recommendations that are made within are done so purely for entertainment value. It is recommended that you always consult a professional prior to undertaking any of the advice or techniques discussed within.

This is a legally binding declaration that is considered both valid and fair by both the Committee of Publishers Association and the American Bar Association and should be considered as legally binding within the United States. The reproduction, transmission, and duplication of any of the content found herein, including any specific or extended information will be done as an illegal act regardless of the end form the information ultimately takes. This includes copied versions of the work both physical, digital and audio unless express consent of the Publisher is provided beforehand. Any additional rights reserved.

Furthermore, the information that can be found within the pages described forthwith shall be considered both accurate and truthful when it comes to the recounting of facts. As such, any use, correct or incorrect, of the provided information will render the Publisher free of responsibility as to the actions taken outside of their direct purview. Regardless, there are zero scenarios where the original author or the Publisher can be deemed liable in any fashion for any damages or hardships that may result from any of the information discussed herein.

Additionally, the information in the following pages is intended only for informational purposes and should thus be thought of as universal. As befitting its nature, it is presented without assurance regarding its prolonged validity or interim quality. Trademarks that are mentioned are done without written consent and can in no way be considered an endorsement from the trademark holder.

Table of Contents

Introduction

Cooking on a pellet grill is a new and unique experience. By utilizing hardwood pellets, the meat product gets infused with a real woodsy, smoky flavor. The new Pellet Smoker Grills can be relied on to do the work on their own, as they are set up to be automatic by the user. The main and most noticeable difference is how they provide the user with an automated air and fuel delivery system, making a pellet grill much easier to control temperatures and relax while doing it.

So, if you thought that smokers are just too difficult to control cooking temperatures, well think again. Pellet grills simply remove the fuss and worry that traditional smokers require, making them virtually a "set it and forget it" way to grill. Pellet grills give you even more as if that were not enough. With your new pellet grill, you have the absolute convenience of combining several varied cooking options. Old-time smokers only smoke their food, so if you want to grill, bake, and roast your food, you would need to purchase separate units for each process.

Pellet Grills are different than propane or gas grills in that they offer more control. Pellet grills and gas grills both offer their own set of convenient features to the outdoor chef but look more closely, and you will see some major differences. Gas grills are very good when cooking chores, but due to poor insulation, they do not typically perform very well at all at low cooking temperatures. Also, the older style of propane grills needs to be set up so that they receive the proper degree of ventilation. This, alone, makes them a poor choice for smokers. The Pellet Grill is a no brainer in today's world!

Pellet grills provide the chef with more flavor options. Pellets are available in many different flavors. This provides you with the ability to cook all the foods on your Pellet Smoker Grill. In the end, sure, they both cook your food, but the pellet grill is exponentially better on so many levels. For me, there is no choice, Pellet Smoker Grill is the best!

Then there is the question of using a Pellet Grill or staying with the highly coveted charcoal method of barbecuing your fine foods.

Charcoal grills have long been considered the king of the backyard barbecue area. There are several choices of configurations for charcoal grills but with two choices for fuel: lump charcoal or charcoal briquettes. Grilling using a charcoal grill is definitely a labor of love. I know several people who defend them to the ends of the earth, and that's fine. We are all different, and thank goodness for that, too. But cooking on a charcoal grill is really not so easy. It takes quite a lot of practice to get all the elements just right and is difficult to control temperatures.

The way pellet grills are used when grilling and smoking is infinitely simpler. This is exactly why they have become the nation's number one seller. As for the cleanup, have you ever seen a charcoal grill the next morning? You may need to carry them out to the trash or recycling. It's not the same with your pellet grill, though. Absolutely simple cleanup is assured for each cooking adventure when you cook with pellets.

Another consideration would be to pit the Pellet Smoker Grills up to the already well-established Electric Smoker available everywhere in the backyard cooking market. Today's electric smokers are actually modern takes on classic smokers and offer lots of control. Electric smokers heat wood chips to get good results. They are quite convenient to operate and allow the chef in your family to set it and forget it. The problem arises when you need to grill and sear. For that, you need very high temperatures, generally between 450 and 550 degrees. Electric smokers do get hot enough for most cooking chores, so it is not all bad news.

Main Characteristics of Smoking

Smoking Meat

Smoking is one of the oldest cooking techniques dating back to the first people living in caves. It was traditionally a food preservation method and with the time, its popularity never died. Smoking is a related process of barbecue. It's the best cooking method to bring out the rich and deep flavor of meat that tastes heavenly when meat is smoked until it comes off the bone.

During smoking, food is cooked below 200 degrees F cooking temperature. Therefore, smoking food requires a lot of time and patience. It infuses woody flavor into the meat and turns a silky and fall-of-bone meat. There are three ways to smoke food, cold smoke, hot smoke and adding liquid smoke. In these three types of smoking methods, liquid smoke is becoming increasingly common. Its main advantage is that smoke flavor is controlled. In addition, the effect of liquid smoke on meat is immediate.

There is another smoking method which called water smoking. It uses water smoker which is specifically designed to incorporate water in the smoking process. The water helps in controlling the temperature of smoker which is great for large cut meats for long hours.

Equipment: A closed container or high-tech smoker.

Fueling: The container will need an external source for a smoke. Wood chips are burn to add smoky flavor to the meat. However, the frequent check should be made to monitor and adjust temperature for smoking.
Best to smoke: A big cut of meats like Briskets, whole chicken, pork, and ribs.
Temperature: 68 to 176 degrees F
Timing: 1 hour to 2 weeks

The Core Elements of Smoking

There are six essential elements of smoking.
1- **Wood chips:** Chip of woods is used as a fuel either alone or in combination with charcoals. In addition, these chips add fantastic flavor to the meat. Therefore, chips of wood should only be used which suits best to the meat.
2- **Smoker:** There are basically four choices from which a smoker should be the pick. The choices are an electric smoker, charcoal smoker, gas smoker and pellet smoker. Each has its own advantages and downsides.
3- **Smoking time:** Smoking time is essential for perfect of meat cuts. It is actually the time when the internal temperature reaches its desired values. It may take 2 hours up to more than two weeks.
4- **Meat**: The star of the show is meat that needs to be more tender, juicy and flavorful after smoking. make sure, the meat has fat trimmed from it. In addition, it should complement the wood of chips.
5- **Rub:** Rubs, mixture or salt and spices, add sweetness and heat to the meat. They should be prepared in such a way that all types of flavor should be balanced in the meat.

6- **Mops:** Mops or liquid is often used during smoking meat. It adds a little bit flavors to the meat and maintains tenderness and moisture throughout the smoking process.

The Core Difference between Cold and Hot Smoking

There are two ways to smoke meat that is cold smoking and hot smoking. In cold smoking, meat is cooked between 68 to 86 degrees F until smoked but moist. It is a good choice to smoke meat like chicken breast, steak, beef, pork chops, salmon, and cheese. The cold smoking concern with adding flavor to the meat rather than cooking. Therefore, when the meat is cold smoked, it should be cured, baked or steamed before serving. On the other hand, hot smoking cooks the meat completely, in addition, to enhance its flavor. Therefore, meat should be a cook until its internal temperature is between 126 to 176 degrees F. Don't let meat temperature reach 185 degrees F as at this temperature, meat shrinks or buckles. Large meat cuts like brisket, ham, ribs and pulled pork turns out great when hot smoked.

Main Characteristics of Pellet Smokers

Components

In order to grasp how an appliance works, it is imperative to know the components of that appliance and what each part does which is what will be doing in this part of the book. This is where we will be examining some of the characteristic features of the wood pellet grill which distinguishes it from the traditional grills and makes it more efficient and reliable. Generally, the entire appliance is made from Stainless Steel due to its durability and resistance to rust or degradation. Also, with Stainless steel, especially in the part of the grill where the actual cooking is done, the grill has better and superior heat retention and consistent temperatures irrespective of weather conditions. Invariably, it never overheats nor degrades with use while at the same time; it is easy to clean after use. Below are the components of a wood pellet grill:

1. **The Lid**

This covers the cooking area where the food is placed which prevents it from being contaminated while being used and when not in use. It is also the part that helps to trap the heat within the cooking area so that the food can have that smoky flavor and taste.

2. **The Burn Pot**

This is where the food is placed for the actual cooking to take place. It is the point where the heat generated in the appliance is directed to for the cooking of the food. Without this part, there will be no juicy and tasty food for consumption.

3. **Temperature Control**

Also known as intelligence temperature control (ITC), it automatically regulates the temperature to the desired degree to suit the kind of food you are cooking and the expected result.

4. **Convection Fan System**

This component of the wood pellet grill supplies airflow to the burning wood pellets, which subsequently generates its heat. Furthermore, a Convection fan system functions for even distribution of heat throughout the grill thus producing tender and juicy cooked food.

5. **Wheels**

These serve the function of mobility which makes it easy to move the grill around in your house especially in your backyard. The wheel can only be rendered non-functional when you decide to mount it in a permanent position but at least, if you do change your mind at some point and decide to move it, it will not be a problem because the source of mobility is already available. It also allows you to keep it in a covered area when it is not in use.

6. **Wood Pellet Hopper**

This is the part where the wood pellets are placed and the size is determined by the speed of cooking you chose to go with. If for example, you prefer cooking meat slowly for long hours, then a hopper with a large size would be more suitable for your needs.

7. **Cold Smokers**

This is an extra feature added by some companies when you purchase wood fire pellet grills and these cold smokers are useful for preparing cheese and salmon dishes.

Pellets

Pellets, classified as biomass, have the shape of small cylinders created by pressing wood waste with special plants, allowing the binding through lignin, the constituent substance of wood, without the addition of additives, solvents and glues harmful to human health and the environment.
Following the pressing process, the pellets, while still hot, are cut to the desired length and passed to the cooling process in special compartments, at the end of which the pellets are sifted through dust and remains, to ensure a percentage not exceeding 1% according to current regulations.
It is precisely the pressing process that gives the pellets a double energy density compared to natural wood, generating the property of higher caloric yield and optimal combustion, whose ashes can still be used as fertilizers, further renewing the process of exploitation of the energy resource.
If you desire to make your own fuel, learn how to make wood pellets.

Choose the Right Raw Material
Before enjoying a beautiful outbreak quietly installed in front of your pellet stove, it will start by choosing the material that will compose your pellets.
Pellets are made from wood residues and waste, until then you are not taught anything.
To make your pellets you need wood, you can use any kind of wood. It can be herbs, peanuts, bamboo, alfalfa, corn stalks, coconut, tree branches or a mix of all that!

The Wood:
It is important to take into account the dimensions of crushing accepted by the press that you have chosen. You may have to pass the wood several times in the mill to obtain residues of suitable size. The moisture substance, preferably, should be close to 12%.

The advantage is that you can use any kind of wood except of course woods from softwoods such as fir. As with chimneys, it is strongly discouraged to burn softwoods as this will clog your pellet stove and increase the risk of fire.
This machine view from above allows observing the principle of operation. A mill turns and compresses wood waste on a perforated plate. Thanks to the change of this one, we can play on the diameter and the shape of the granule (from 0.8mm to 8mm).
We can use this machine for making pet kibbles.

The Material Needed To Make Pellets:
Now that you have shredded your branches and other pieces of wood, here is the material you will need to make your pellets.
Most importantly, the pellet press.
It can be turn wood into pellets. You will find at all prices, from 1000 to over 3000 $ and sometimes even used.
If you are handyman you can even start manufacturing your own pellet machine.
Finally, a hygrometer will be very useful for checking the moisture content during the drying stage of the milled wood.

The Steps to Make Your Pellets:

1. Grinding the wood with the woodchipper:

First you have to grind the wood. It is advisable to use a woodchipper which has the possibility to work with a calibration grid to produce a crusher having the dimensions adapted to the pellet press.

2. Make a second grinding:

The product resulting from the first grinding must be introduced again into the crusher.

3. Tumble dry:

Since the wood to be chopped must be green, it will be necessary to let dry the product obtained after the second grinding before any use. We recall that the optimum moisture content for a compact pellet is between 10 and 14%.
Once the ground material is dry, it must be introduced into the hopper of the press to turn it into pellet.

A process accessible to everyone?
Not everyone can make pellets, starting with those who live in the city. Difficult to recover wood while it is already a rare raw material in our streets!
It is therefore a process rather intended for pellet stove owners who have the ability to recover the type of wood branching easily.
And that's without forgetting the place it takes to store the machine and to dry the wood, which can be a little complicated in a Parisian 50sqm.
Making your own wood pellets, is it really economical?
If all the conditions are met for the manufacture of pellets, (machine bought at a good price and wood supply) then yes, this is really economical.
In addition, it is an ecological approach because it allows recycling green waste from your garden to turn them into natural fuel.

How to Store Pellet Wood Indoors?
Bags sold in supermarkets or specialized stores are dotted with micro holes. It is effective in reducing humidity but to a certain extent.
That's why, the granule box team to develop a pellet storage design for the interior of the house. With different capacities ranging from 30kg to 55kg of wood pellets, the pellet storage fits easily into the living room. The pellet storage is made of steel with a sheet of first choice and provided by high-resistance epoxy paint. For some models, the pellet storage is equipped with a tempered glass window 4mm thick.

What Are The Advantages Of Storing Its Pellets In A Granule Box?
Beyond the aesthetic point of view of pellet storage imagined by some team, the granule box has several significant advantages.
Place wood pellet storage next to your wood pellet stove:
- Dramatically reduce the moisture content unfortunately still present in your wood pellet
- By reducing the humidity, the heat output of your pellet stove wood will be more important.

- Storing 55kg of wood pellets, avoids you going back and forth between your wood pellet stove and the saddler or garage of your house.

Main Smokers on the Market

Electric Smokers

The electric smoker is the best smoker because it is very simple to use. Just set it, put your food in it and leave the rest of the work to the smoker. There is nothing an electric smoker can't grill, be it seafood, poultry, meat, cheese or bread. It requires little attention unlike other smokers like filling water bin, lighting wood or charcoal and checking on fuel frequently. Yes, unlike traditional smoker, electric smoker just need 2 to 4 ounce of wood chips that turns out a delicious and flavorful smoky food. Furthermore, they maintain cooking temperature really well. On the other hand, it sleek and stylish look and small size make it appropriate if you are living in an apartment or condo. Due to their simpler functions and hassle-free cooking, the electric smoker is a good choice for beginner cooks who want to get started with smoking food.

Gas Smokers

Gas smokers or propane smoker are much like a gas grill using propane as a fuel. Therefore, the heat for cooking remains consistent and steady. Furthermore, gas smokers are as easy to use, just set the temperature and walk away. However, frequent checks need to be done to make sure fuel doesn't run out. It isn't a big issue but one should keep in mind. And the best part, a gas smoker can be used when there is no electricity or when you need an oven. A gas smoker can take up to cooking temperature to 450 degrees, making this smoker flexible to be used as an oven. Another fantastic feature of gas smoker is its portability so they can use anywhere. Just pack it and take it along with you on your camping trips or other outdoor adventures.

Charcoal Smokers

Nothing can beat the flavor charcoal gives to your food. Its best flavor just simply can't match with any other smoker flavor. Unfortunately, setting a charcoal smoker, tuning fuel, maintaining cooking temperature and checking food can be a pain and you might burn the food. Not to worry, these hassles of a charcoal smoker does go away with practice and experience. Therefore, a charcoal smoker suits perfectly for serious grillers and barbecue purist who want flavors.

Pellet Smokers

Pellet smokers are making a surge due to their best feature of a pallet of maintaining a consistent temperature. It contains an automated system to drop pallets which frees the cook to monitor fuel level. The addition of thermostat gives the user the complete control the cooking temperature and grilling of food under ideal condition. In addition, the smoking food uses the heat from hardwood which gives food a delicious flavor. The only downside of pallet smoker is their high cost between the ranges of $100 to %600.

Wood Pellet Smoker Manufacturer

Just a few years ago, wood pellet smoker grill makers were only a handful. At this time, there are more than 20 and divide them into 3 groups: entry-level, mid-level, and high-end units. On the manufacturer websites, you will find evaluations, videos, and articles and so on that will support you determine which smoker grill best suits your needs. There are also forums and blogs on wood pellet smokers-only grills.

Here are some of the wood pellet smoker grill makers

- England stove works
- Green Mountain Grill
- Fahrenheit Technologies Inc. (Grilla)
- IPT pellet grill
- Louisiana Grill
- MAK grill
- Memphis grill
- Ozark Mountain Pellet Grill
- Pellet Pro
- Rec Tec grill
- Royall Wood Pellet Grills

Not all wood pellet smoker grill manufacturers choose to test their units in the forums. This is not to blame these manufacturers because those units are based on their own benefits.

Advantages of Using Pellets

Before starting to use your Wood Pellet for the first time, and before getting started with some of the most sumptuous recipes you can ever stumble into, here are some of the most important things you need to know about Wood Pellets at first. Indeed, Wood pellets are basically a form of compressed wood and of sawdust that is basically created through the process of exposing certain agents to a certain degree of heat. And one of the most well-known uses of wood pellets is to use it in order to fuel certain cooking smokers and grills. Wood Pellet Smokers and Grills are indeed, known for bringing a very special smoked flavor of wood to the food ingredients you are smoking or to any type of meat. And the smoking taste that you can get from wood pellet smokers is very special and unique that you can never forget the taste of food once you try smoke cooking it with the Wood Pellet Smoker or Grill. And before starting your wood pellet journey, here are some tips of using Wood Pellet Smoker or Grills, in addition to some benefits of Wood Pellet cooking:

Eco-Friendly

Wood pellets are mainly characterized by being eco-friendly; basically because most of the Wood Pellets are made of renewable elements and materials. The production of Wood Pellets encourages on the process of repurposing the materials that can be thrown away by people.

Efficient
Wood pellets are known for being a lot more efficient in comparison to other types of gas and fossil because wood pellets are mainly able to use about 90% of the contained energy. And then the wood pellets can turn the energy into heat.

Cheap
You can use a pellet tube smoker in order to keep wood pellets in as you combine it with the charcoal. And this can help increase the smokiness of the flavor. Pellet tube smokers are usually affordable and are worth to check it out.

Versatility
There is no denying thru fact that the amount and mammoth variety of food that you can prepare on a wood pellet grill is incredible. Regardless of whether it is beef, pork, chicken, baking dishes or more; you can have all of it in the grill which makes it a very versatile choice.

Quick
The overall design is such that the whole thing is ready in 10 to 15 minutes and when you compare it with other devices to cook food, the speed of cooking is much improved.

Even cooking
To get the best cooking flavor and taste, the food must be cooked evenly. The wood pellet grills are so designed that the smoke effect will be cleared and the smoke spreads evenly thereby giving your food the perfectly evened out cooking taste.

The flavors
Like we have mentioned before, wood pellet grill is known to lend a characteristic flavor of their own. When you use these pellets, you are sure to enjoy the flavor that will give your food a twist you are going to absolutely love.

Temperature regulation

When you are cooking food, needing to regulate the temperature is an absolute must. There is no denying the fact that we all need to keep a watchful eye on the temperature with this kind of grill. It is a whole lot easier to monitor the heat and the temperature which has generated.

So, these are the umpteen benefits that the wood pellet grill smokers have to offer. No doubt, they enjoy an astounding level of popularity and before you get ahead with some of the most lip-smacking recipes in the book, we want you to find yourself one of the perfect wood pellet grills. Trust us; barbecuing would be so much more fun than you will wish to host a BBQ party every weekend and call your friends over!

Make sure to go through the specifics well, understand the details, and then get yourself a grill you will love to cook on. The smoked effect and the extra infusion of flavor are going to help you earn the title of the most coveted chef. Trust me; you need a wood pellet grill in your backyard right away!

The Basic Preparations for Smoking Meat

Choosing Smoker

The major and foremost step is to choose a smoker. You can invest in any type of the smoker: charcoal smoker, gas smoker or an electric smoker. A charcoal smoker runs for a long time and maintains steadier heat in the smoker and give meat pure flavors. A good choice for beginner cook for smoking meat is a gas smoker where there is no need to monitor temperature but it comes with a downside that meat won't have much flavor compared to charcoal. On the other hand, the simplest, easiest and popular smoker is an electric smoker. Cooking with electric smoker involves only two-step: turn it on, put meat in it and walk away.

Choosing Fuel

Wood chips add a unique flavor to the meat, therefore, select that wood chips that would enhance the taste of meat. Some wood of chips has a stronger flavor, some have mild while others are just enough to be alone for smoking.

Type of Smoking Method

You have two choices to smoke meat, either using wet smoking, dry smoking, liquid smoke or water smoking.

Soaking Chips of Wood

Wood chips need to soak in order to last longer for fueling smoking. The reason is dry wood that burns quickly and this means, adding fuel to the smoker which can result in dry smoked meat. There isn't any need of using wood chips when smoking for a shorter time. Prepare wood chips by soaking them in water for at least 4 hours before starting smoking. Then drain chips and wrap and seal them in an aluminum foil. Use toothpick or fork for poking holes into the wood chips bag.

Set Smoker

Each type of smoker has its own way to start smoking. For wood or charcoal smoker, first, light up half of the charcoals and wait until their flame goes down. Then add remaining charcoal and wood chips if using. Wait they are lighted and giving heat completely, then push charcoal aside and place meat on the other side of grilling grate. This is done to make sure that meat is indirectly smoked over low heat. Continue adding charcoal and/or soaked wood chips into the smoker.
For gas/propane or electric smoker, just turn it on according to manufacturer guideline and then add soaked wood chips into chip holder and fill water receptacle if a smoker has one. Either make use of the incorporated thermostat or buy your own to monitor the internal temperature of the smoker. When smoker reaches to desired preheated temperature, add meat to it.

Selecting Meat for Smoking

Choose the type of meat which tastes good with a smoky flavor. Following meat goes well for smoking.
Beef: ribs, brisket and corned beef.
Pork: spare ribs, roast, shoulder, and ham.
Poultry: whole chicken, whole turkey, and big game hens.
Seafood: Salmon, scallops, trout, and lobster.

Getting the Meat Ready

Prepare meat according to the recipe. Sometimes meat is cured, marinated or simply seasoned with the rub. These preparation methods ensure smoked meat turn out flavorful, tender and extremely juicy.
Brine is a solution to treating poultry, pork or ham. It involves dissolving brine ingredients in water poured into a huge container and then adding meat to it. Then let soak for at least 8 hours and after that, rinse it well and pat dry before you begin smoking.
Marinate treat beef or briskets and add flavors to it. It's better to make deep cuts in meat to let marinate ingredients deep into it. Drain meat or smoke it straightaway.
Rubs are commonly used to treat beef, poultry or ribs. They are actually a combination of salt and many spices, rubbed generously all over the meat. Then the meat is left to rest for at least 2 hours or more before smoking it.
Before smoking meat, make sure it is at room temperature. This ensures meat is cooked evenly and reaches its internal temperature at the end of smoking time.

Placing Meat into the Smoker

Don't place the meat directly over heat into the smoker because the main purpose of smoking is cooking meat at low temperature. Set aside your fuel on one side of the smoker and place meat on the other side and let cook.
Smoking time: The smoking time of meat depends on the internal temperature. For this, use a meat thermometer and insert it into the thickest part of the meat. The smoking time also varies with the size of meat. Check recipes to determine the exact smoking time for the meat.

Basting Meat

Some recipes call for brushing meat with thin solutions, sauces or marinade. This step not only makes meat better in taste, it also helps to maintain moisture in meat through the smoking process. Read recipe to check out if basting is necessary.
Taking out meat: When the meat reaches its desired internal temperature, remove it from the smoker. Generally, poultry should be removed from smoker when its internal temperature reaches to 165 degrees F. For ground meats, ham, and pork, the internal temperature should be 160 degrees F. 145 degrees F is the internal temperature for chops, roast, and steaks.

Choose the Right Preferred Wood Pellet

Smoker Preferred Wood Pellet is an important element which you need to decide correctly to cook a delicious smoked food. The reason is that smoker chips of Preferred Wood Pellets impart different flavors on the food you are cooking in the smoker. Therefore, you should know which smoker Preferred Wood Pellet should be used to create a delicious smoked food. Here is the lowdown of smoker Preferred Wood Pellets and which food is best with them.

1. **Alder:** A lighter smoker Preferred Wood Pellet with natural sweetness.

Best to smoke: Any fish especially salmon, poultry, and game birds.

2. **Maple:** This smoker preferred Wood Pellet has a mild and sweet flavor. In addition, its sweet smoke gives the food a dark appearance. For better flavor, use it as a combination with alder, apple, or oak smoker Preferred Wood Pellets.

Best to smoke: Vegetables, cheese, and poultry.

3. **Apple:** A mild fruity flavor smoker Preferred Wood Pellet with natural sweetness. When mixed with oak smoker Preferred Wood Pellet, it gives a great flavor to food. Let food smoke for several hours as the smoke takes a while to permeate the food with the flavors.

Best to smoke: Poultry, beef, pork, lamb, and seafood.

4. **Cherry:** This smoker Preferred Wood Pellet is an all-purpose fruity flavor Preferred Wood Pellet for any type of meat. Its smoke gives the food a rich, mahogany color. Try smoking by mixing it with alder, oak, pecan, and hickory smoker Preferred Wood Pellet.

Best to smoke: Chicken, turkey, ham, pork, and beef.

5. **Oak:** Oak Preferred Wood Pellet gives a medium flavor to food which is stronger compared to apple Preferred Wood Pellet and cherry Preferred Wood Pellet and lighter compared to hickory. This versatile smoker Preferred Wood Pellet works well blended with hickory, apple, and cherry Preferred Wood Pellets.

Best to smoke: Sausages, brisket, and lamb.

6. **Peach and Pear:** Both smoker Preferred Wood Pellets are like each other. They give food a subtle light and fruity flavor with the addition of natural sweetness.

Best to smoke: Poultry, pork, and game birds.

7. **Hickory:** Hickory Preferred Wood Pellet infuses a strong sweet and bacon flavor into the food, especially meat cuts. Do not over smoke with this Preferred Wood Pellet as it can turn the taste of food bitter.

Best to smoke: Red meat, poultry, pork shoulder, ribs.

8. **Pecan:** This sweet smoker Preferred Wood Pellet lends the food a rich and nutty flavor. Use it with Mesquite Preferred Wood Pellet to balance its sweetness.

Best to smoke: Poultry, pork.

9. **Walnut:** This strong flavored smoker Preferred Wood Pellet is often used as a mixing Preferred Wood Pellet due to its slightly bitter flavor. Use walnut Preferred Wood Pellet with lighter smoke Preferred Wood Pellets like pecan Preferred Wood Pellet or apple Preferred Wood Pellet.

Best to smoke: Red meat and game birds.

10. **Grape:** Grape Preferred Wood Pellet chips give a sweet berry flavor to food. It is best to use these Preferred Wood Pellet chips with apple Preferred Wood Pellet chips.

Best to smoke: Poultry

11. **Mulberry:** Mulberry Preferred Wood Pellet chips are like apple Preferred Wood Pellet chips. It adds natural sweetness and gives berry finish to the food.

Best to smoke: Ham and Chicken.

12. **Mesquite:** Mesquite Preferred Wood Pellet chips flavor is earthy and slightly harsh and bitter. It burns fast and strongly hot. Therefore, do not use it for longer grilling.

Best to smoke: Red meat, dark meat.

Selecting the Meat

Choose the type of meat which tastes good with a smoky flavor. Following meat goes well for smoking.
Beef: ribs, brisket, and corned beef.
Pork: spareribs, roast, shoulder, and ham.
Poultry: whole chicken, whole turkey, and big game hens.
Seafood: Salmon, scallops, trout, and lobster.

Find the Right Smoke Temperature

There are two ways to smoke meat that is cold smoking and hot smoking. In cold smoking, meat is cooked between 68 to 86 degrees F until smoked but moist. It is a good choice to smoke meat like chicken breast, steak, beef, pork chops, salmon, and cheese. The cold smoking concern with adding flavor to the meat rather than cooking. Therefore, when the meat is cold smoked, it should be cured, baked, or steamed before serving.

On the other hand, hot smoking cooks the meat completely, in addition, to enhance its flavor. Therefore, meat should be a cook until its internal Smoke Temperature is between 126 to 176 degrees F. Does not let meat Smoke Temperature reach 185 degrees F as at this Smoke Temperature, meat shrinks or buckles? Large meat cuts like brisket, ham, ribs and pulled pork turns out great when hot smoked.

FTC

This important abbreviation is Foil-Towel-Cooler and is a popular method used to preserve and/or rest cooked meat, like pork thighs, breasts and turkey, for redistributing the juice in the meat. It produces a moist and gentle end product. Pitmasters, professionals, catering companies and restaurants, for example, use industrial units such as Cambro to achieve these results. The FTC is affectionately known as the Cambro poor.
Wrap the cooked meat in strong aluminum foil to hold the juice. Wrap the meat inside a huge towel before placing it in the ice chest. If you wish, reduce the air space by filling the refrigerator with towels to prevent heat dissipation. Pork legs and chest FTC in a closed refrigerator for at least 2 hour and up to 4 to 6 hour, based on the meat... Be careful when handling meat, as it will still be too hot to eat, even after a few hours of rest.

Poultry Recipes

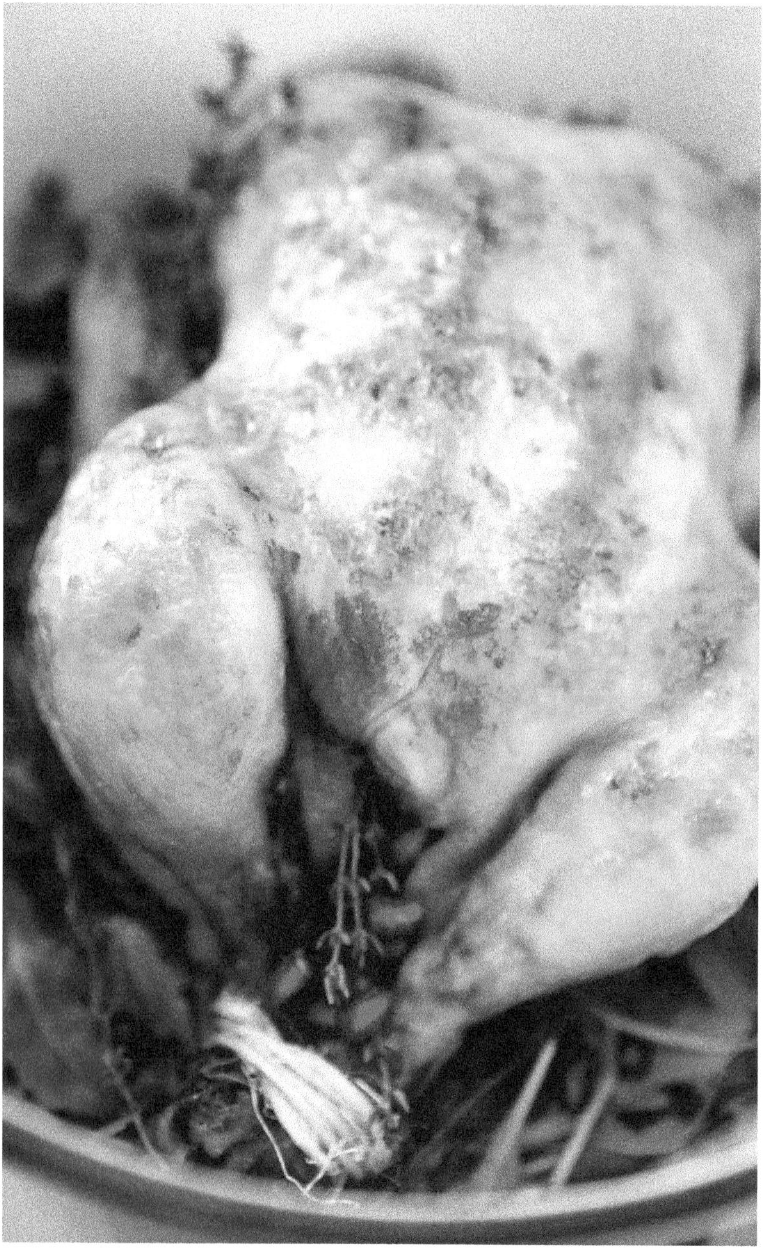

Citrus Flavored Goose Breast

Preparation Time: 6 hours
Cooking Time: 40 minutes
Servings: 6
Smoke Temperature: **300**°F
Ingredients:
½ a cup of orange juice
1/3 cup of olive oil
1/3 cup of Dijon mustard
1/3 cup of brown sugar
¼ cup of soy sauce
¼ cup of honey
1 tablespoon of dried minced onion
1 teaspoon of garlic powder
8 goose breast halves
1 cup of soaked hickory wood chips
Directions:
Take a medium sized bowl and whisk in the orange juice, mustard, olive oil, soy sauce, sugar onion, and honey and garlic powder. Mix the marinade well.
Place the goose in the marinade and cover it up.
Let it refrigerate for about 3-6 hours. Preheat your smoker to a temperature of 300 degrees Fahrenheit. Add some soaked hickory wood chips to create added smoke.
Place the breasts on the grate and brush them up occasionally with the marinade for the first 30 minutes.
Smoke them until the juices run clear and the breast reaches an internal temperature of 165 degrees Fahrenheit.

Nutrition: Calories: 1094 Protein: 32g Carbs: 14g Fat: 64g

Smoked Brown Sugar Turkey

Preparation Time: 15 minutes
Cooking Time: 8 hours
Servings: 6
Smoke Temperature: 180°F
Ingredients:
2 lbs. Turkey breast
4 cups Cold water
¼ cup Salt
1 cup Brown sugar
2 tbsp. Garlic powder
1 tbsp. Sea salt
1 tbsp. Cayenne pepper
2 tbsp. dried onions
2 tbsps. Sugar
2 tbsps. Chili powder
2 tbsps. Black pepper
2 tbsps. Cumin
¼ cup Paprika
2 tbsps. Brown sugar
Directions:
In a large enough bowl, mix together all of the brine ingredients except the turkey.
Add the turkey and cover with brine properly. Put this bowl in your refrigerator for about 15–20 hours.
Remove the turkey from the mixture of brine.
Prepare your Wood Pellet Smoker-Grill by preheating it to a temperature of about 180°F. Close the lid for about 15 minutes before adding the turkey.
Prepare the BBQ rub with the provided ingredients and coat the turkey properly.
Transfer this seasoned turkey straight to the grilling grate.
Allow for about 6–8 hours of smoking to get an internal temperature of about 160°F.
Remove the smoked turkey from your smoker-grill and allow it to rest for at least 10 minutes.

Nutrition: *Calories: 155 Protein: 29g Carbs: 8g Fat: 3g*

Whole Turkey

Preparation Time: 30 minutes
Cooking Time: 6 hours
Servings: 8
Smoke Temperature: 250°F
Ingredients:
Two t. thyme
Two t. sage
½ c. apple juice
One stick melted butter
¼ c. poultry seasoning
EVOO
10-12 pound turkey
Directions:
Add wood pellets to your smoker and follow your cooker's startup procedure. Preheat your smoker, with your lid closed, until it reaches 250.
Rub the oil and seasoning on the turkey. Get some in under the skin as well as inside.
Mix the thyme, sage, juice, and butter together.
Place the turkey in a roasting pan, put it on the grill, cover, and cook 5-6 hours. Baste it every hour with the juice mixture.
It should reach 165. Let it rest for 15-20 minutes before carving.

Nutrition: *Calories: 48.2 Protein: 8.3g Carbs: 0.3g Fat: 1.4g*

Pineapple Turkey Wings

Preparation Time: 30 minutes
Cooking Time: 6 hours
Servings: 6
Smoke Temperature: **350**°F and 165°F
Ingredients:
Pepper
Salt
¼ t. garlic powder
Two pounds turkey wings
One T. packed brown sugar
Two t. chili powder
One 11-ounce cans pineapple, undrained
¼ t. ground ginger
One 11-ounce cans tomato sauce
Directions:
Put the turkey wings into a large dish. Make sure they are in one layer. In a bowl, put the pepper, salt, garlic powder, ginger, chili powder, brown sugar, pineapple, and tomato sauce.
This mixture should be poured on the turkey. Place into the refrigerator for four to five hours.
Add wood pellets to your smoker and follow your cooker's startup procedure.
Preheat your smoker, with your lid closed, until it reaches 350.
Take the turkey wings out of the marinade.
Use the paper towels to pat them dry. Place them onto the grill and smoke for 5 minutes on both sides.
Move to cool side and allow to smoke for an additional 40 minutes. Internal temperature needs to be 165.

Nutrition: *Calories: 260 Protein: 31.05g Carbs: 0.1g Fat: 14.1g*

Cheesy Turkey Patties

Preparation Time: 30 minutes
Cooking Time: 1 hour
Servings: 4
Smoke Temperature: 380°F
Ingredients:
Pepper
One t. chili powder
½ avocado
¼ c. light cream cheese
One tomato
¼ c. shredded cheddar
One cucumber
Two t. chopped green onion
One t. oregano
One pound ground turkey
Salt
Directions:
Place the oregano, pepper, salt, and turkey into a bowl.
Mix everything together with your hands. Form into four patties.
Add wood pellets to your smoker and follow your cooker's startup procedure. Preheat your smoker, with your lid closed, until it reaches 380.
Smoke the patties on the grill. Each side should take approximately five minutes.
While patties are cooking, mix together the cheddar cheese, cream cheese, chili powder, green onion, and salt.
Slice the pita bread open and spread the mixture onto the inside of the pita.
Place a turkey patty inside along with cucumber, tomato, and avocado slices.

Nutrition: *Calories: 217 Protein: 25.3g Carbs: 0g Fat: 12.16g*

Barbecue Chicken Breasts

Preparation Time: 20 minutes
Cooking Time: 30 minutes
Servings: 4
Smoke Temperature: 350°F
Ingredients:
Two T. Worcestershire sauce
½ c. hot barbecue sauce
One c. barbecue sauce
Two cloves minced garlic
¼ c. olive oil
4 chicken breasts
Directions:
Put the chicken breasts into a deep container.
In another bowl, put the Worcestershire sauce, barbecue sauces, garlic, and olive oil. Stir well to combine.
Use half to marinate the chicken and reserve the rest for basting.
Add wood pellets to your smoker and follow your cooker's startup procedure. Preheat your smoker, with your lid closed, until it reaches 350.
Take the chicken breasts out of the sauce. On the grill, place them before smoking them for approximately 20 minutes.
About ten minutes before the chicken is finished, baste with reserved barbecue sauce.

Nutrition: *Calories: 220 Protein: 27g Carbs: 19g Fat: 3.3g*

Master Tip: Using a syringe to inject broth into the breast meat before cooking makes it softer and more succulent

Cilantro-Lime Chicken

Preparation Time: 50 minutes
Cooking Time: 5 hours
Servings: 4
Smoke Temperature: 350°F
Ingredients:
Pepper
Salt
4 cloves minced garlic
½ c. lime juice
One c. honey
Two T. olive oil
½ c. chopped cilantro
4 chicken breasts
Directions:
Put the chicken breasts into a large zip-top bag.
In another bowl, put the pepper, salt, olive oil, garlic, honey, lime juice, and cilantro. Stir well to combine.
Use half as a marinade and reserve the rest for later.
Place into the refrigerator for four to five hours.

Add wood pellets to your smoker and follow your cooker's startup procedure. Preheat your smoker, with your lid closed, until it reaches 350.

Remove the chicken breasts the bag. Use paper towels to pat them dry. Let them smoke up in the grill for about fifteen minutes

Baste with reserved marinade.

Nutrition: *Calories: 62.5 Protein: 8.2g Carbs: 3g Fat: 2g*

Lemon Honey Chicken

Preparation Time: 30 minutes
Cooking Time: 30 minutes
Servings: 4
Smoke Temperature: 350°F
Ingredients:
Pepper
Salt
Chopped rosemary
One clove crushed garlic
One T. honey
Juice of one lemon
½ c. chicken broth
3 T. butter
4 chicken breasts
Directions:
Put a pan over the stove and melt the butter. Place chicken breasts into hot butter and sear on each side until a nice color has formed.
Take out of the pan and allow to rest for ten minutes.
In a small bowl, put the pepper, salt, rosemary, garlic, honey, lemon juice, and broth. Stir well to combine.
Rub each breast with the honey lemon mixture.
Add wood pellets to your smoker and follow your cooker's startup procedure. Preheat your smoker, with your lid closed, until it reaches 350.
Put the chicken breasts onto the preheated grill and grill for 20 minutes.

Nutrition: *Calories: 265.1 Protein: 31.1g Carbs: 25.3g Fat: 7g*

Mediterranean Chicken

Preparation Time: 30 minutes
Cooking Time: 3 hours
Servings: 6
Smoke Temperature: 350°F
Ingredients:
Lemon slices to garnish
Salt
Pepper
One t. chopped rosemary
3 cloves minced garlic
Zest of one lemon
One t. oregano
Small chopped onion
½ c. white wine
¼ c. olive oil
4 chicken breasts
Directions:
Put the chicken breasts into a large zip-top bag.
In another bowl, put the olive oil, white wine, lemon zest, onion, garlic, oregano, rosemary, pepper, and salt. Stir well to combine.
Coat the chicken in this mixture. Place into the refrigerator for two to three hours.
Add wood pellets to your smoker and follow your cooker's startup procedure. Preheat your smoker, with your lid closed, until it reaches 350.
The chicken breast should be removed from the bag before patting them dry with paper towels. Place them on the grill and smoke for 15 minutes.
Leave it for 10 minutes before slicing. Garnish with sliced lemon.

Nutrition: *Calories: 330.6 Protein: 57.3g Carbs: 15.1g Fat: 3.6g*

Spicy Chicken Thighs

Preparation Time: 45 minutes
Cooking Time: 4 hours
Servings: 6
Smoke Temperature: 350°F
Ingredients:
One T. dry barbecue spice
One t. coriander
One T. oregano
1/3 c. balsamic vinegar
Two T. mustard
1/3 c. olive oil
Pepper
Two cloves minced garlic
6 chicken thighs
Directions:
Put the chicken thighs into a shallow dish in one layer.
In a bowl, put the dry barbecue spice, coriander, oregano, pepper, salt, mustard, olive oil, balsamic vinegar, and garlic. Stir well to combine.
Use the mixture to coat the chicken.
Place into the refrigerator for four hours.
Add wood pellets to your smoker and follow your cooker's startup procedure. Preheat your smoker, with your lid closed, until it reaches 350.
Remove the thighs of the chicken from the dish and use paper towels to pat them dry.
Place them onto the preheated grill with the skin down and smoke for ten minutes each side.

Nutrition: Calories: 479 Protein: 22g Carbs: 20g Fat: 35g

Red Pepper Chicken Thighs

Preparation Time: 45 minutes
Cooking Time: 4 hours
Servings: 6
Smoke Temperature: 450°F
Ingredients:
One T. garlic powder
One t. curry powder
One t. red pepper flakes
One t. black pepper
Two T. olive oil
½ c. chicken broth
One t. oregano
One t. paprika
Two pounds chicken thighs
Directions:
Put the chicken thighs into a large flat dish in a single layer.
In a bowl, put and stir the olive oil, garlic powder, curry, oregano, pepper, paprika, red pepper flakes, and broth.
Pour on top of the chicken.
Let the chicken marinate for four hours.
Add wood pellets to your smoker and follow your cooker's startup procedure. Preheat your smoker, with your lid closed, until it reaches 450.
The chicken thighs should be removed from the bag. Use paper towels to pat them dry.
Place them onto the preheated grill with the skin down and smoke for ten minutes each side.

Nutrition: *Calories: 213.8 Protein: 43g Carbs: 0.6g Fat: 2.3g*

Herbed Coffee Chicken

Preparation Time: 40 minutes
Cooking Time: 2 hours
Servings: 4
Smoke Temperature: 350°F
Ingredients:
Salt
¾ c. strong brewed coffee
One t. coriander seeds
4 lemon slices
One t. peppercorns
One t. mustard seeds
½ c. chicken broth
¼ c. dark brown sugar, packed
Two T. melted butter
4 chicken breast halves
Directions:
Rub the butter on the chicken and rub in the salt.
In a large container, stir together the remaining ingredients. Cover the chicken with marinade.
Place into the refrigerator for two hours.
Add wood pellets to your smoker and follow your cooker's startup procedure. Preheat your smoker, with your lid closed, until it reaches 350.
Smoke the chicken for ten minutes.

Nutrition: *Calories: 127 Protein: 26.3g Carbs: 0.5g Fat: 1.5g*

Game Recipes

Cornish Game Hens

Preparation Time: 10 minutes
Cooking Time: 1 hour
Servings: 6
Smoke Temperature: 375°F and 165°F
Ingredients:
4 Cornish game hens, giblets removed
4 teaspoons chicken rub
4 sprigs of rosemary
4 tablespoons butter, unsalted, melted
Directions:
Switch on the grill, fill the grill hopper with mesquite flavored wood pellets, power the grill on by using the control panel, select 'smoke' on the temperature dial, or set the temperature to 375 degrees F and let it preheat for a minimum of 15 minutes.
Meanwhile, rinse the hens, pat dry with paper towels, tie the wings by using a butcher's strong, then rub evenly with melted butter, sprinkle with chicken rub and stuff cavity of each hen with a rosemary sprig.
When the grill has preheated, open the lid, place hens on the grill grate, shut the grill, and smoke for 1 hour until thoroughly cooked and internal temperature reaches 165 degrees F.
When done, transfer hens to a dish, let rest for 5 minutes and then serve.

Nutrition: Calories: 173 Cal Fat: 7.4 g Carbs: 1 g Protein: 24.1 g Fiber: 0.2 g

BBQ Elk Short Ribs

Preparation Time: 10 minutes
Cooking Time: 1 hour
Servings: 6
Smoke Temperature: **450**°F and 275°F
Ingredients:
1/2 pound green beans
3 pounds elk short ribs
1/2 pound chanterelle mushrooms
6 ounces rib rub
Salt as needed
Ground black pepper as needed
4 tablespoons unsalted butter
Directions:
Switch on the grill, fill the grill hopper with cherry flavored wood pellets, power the grill on by using the control panel, select 'smoke' on the temperature dial, or set the temperature to 275 degrees F and let it preheat for a minimum of 15 minutes.
Meanwhile, prepare the ribs, and for this, season them with salt and rib rub until well coated.
When the grill has preheated, open the lid, place ribs on the grill grate rib-side down, shut the grill and smoke for 30 minutes.
Then wrap ribs in foil in the double layer, return to the grill grate and continue smoking 15 minutes or until the internal temperature reaches 125 degrees.
When done, transfer ribs to a dish and let them rest until required.
Change the smoking temperature to 450 degrees F, shut with lid, and let it preheat for 15 minutes.
Then place a skillet pan on the grill grate and when hot, add butter and when it melts, add mushrooms and beans, toss until mixed, shut with lid, and cook for 15 minutes until vegetables have turned tender and golden brown.
Serve grilled vegetables with elk ribs.

Nutrition: *Calories: 393 Cal Fat: 16.6 g Carbs: 25 g Protein: 36 g Fiber: 0.9 g*

Grilled Duck Breast

Preparation Time: 10 minutes
Cooking Time: 20 minutes
Servings: 6
Smoke Temperature: 450°F and 135°F
Ingredients:
4 duck breasts, boneless, each about 6 ounces
1/4 cup game rubs
Directions:
Switch on the grill, fill the grill hopper with cherry flavored wood pellets, power the grill on by using the control panel, select 'smoke' on the temperature dial, or set the temperature to 450 degrees F and let it preheat for a minimum of 15 minutes.
Cut the skin on the breast of the duck, in the form of the ¼-inch diamond pattern by using a sharp knife and then season with game rub until evenly coated.
When the grill has preheated, open the lid, place duck breasts on the grill grate skin-side down, shut the grill and smoke for 20 minutes until cooked and the internal temperature reaches 135 degrees F.
When done, transfer duck breasts to a cutting board, let them rest for 10 minutes, then cut into slices and then serve.
Nutrition: Calories: 220 Cal Fat: 18 g Carbs: 0 g Protein: 16 g Fiber: 0 g

Bison Slider

Preparation Time: 10 minutes
Cooking Time: 8 minutes
Servings: 8
Smoke Temperature: 450°F
Ingredients:
1 pound ground buffalo meat
1 tablespoon minced garlic
1 teaspoon salt
1 teaspoon ground black pepper
2 tablespoons Worcestershire sauce
Directions:
Switch on the Traeger grill, fill the grill hopper with flavored wood pellets, power the grill on by using the control panel, select 'smoke' on the temperature dial, or set the temperature to 450 degrees F and let it preheat for a minimum of 5 minutes.
Meanwhile, take a medium bowl; place all the ingredients in it, stir until well combined, and then shape the mixture into eight patties.
When the grill has preheated, open the lid, place patties on the grill grate, shut the grill and smoke for 4 minutes per side until thoroughly cooked.
Serve patties with toasted buns and favorite toppings.

Nutrition: Calories: 120 Cal Fat: 8 g Carbs: 2 g Protein: 10 g Fiber: 0.6 g

Venison Rib Roast

Preparation Time: 10 minutes
Cooking Time: 25 minutes
Servings: 6
Smoke Temperature: **375**°F and 125°F
Ingredients:
2 pounds venison roast, about 8 ribs
Rib rubs as needed
1 tablespoon olive oil
Directions:
Switch on the grill, fill the grill hopper with hickory flavored wood pellets, power the grill on by using the control panel, select 'smoke' on the temperature dial, or set the temperature to 375 degrees F and let it preheat for a minimum of 5 minutes.
Meanwhile, brush roast with oil and then season with rib rub until well coated.
When the grill has preheated, open the lid, place food on the grill grate, shut the grill, and smoke for 25 minutes until the internal temperature reaches 125 degrees F.
When done, transfer roast to a cutting board, leave it for at least 10 minutes, then cut into slices and serve.

Nutrition: *Calories: 128 Cal Fat: 2.8 g Carbs: 0 g Protein: 24.8 g Fiber: 0 g*

Venison Meatloaf

Preparation Time: 30 minutes
Cooking Time: 1 hour and 15 minutes
Servings: 6
Smoke Temperature: **350**°F and 165°F
Ingredients:
For the Meatloaf:
1 medium white onion, peeled, diced
2 pounds ground venison
1 cup bread crumbs
1 teaspoon salt

1 tablespoon Worcestershire sauce
½ teaspoon ground black pepper
2 tablespoons onion soup mix
1 egg, beaten
1 cup milk, unsweetened
For the Glaze:
1/4 cup brown sugar
1/4 cup ketchup
1/4 cup apple cider vinegar

Directions:

Switch on the Traeger grill, fill the grill hopper with big game blend wood pellets, power the grill on by using the control panel, select 'smoke' on the temperature dial, or set the temperature to 350 degrees F and let it preheat for a minimum of 15 minutes.

Meanwhile, take a large bowl, place all the ingredients for the meatloaf in it, and stir until just combined; don't over mix.

Take a loaf pan, grease it with oil, place meatloaf mixture in it, and spread evenly.

Prepare the glaze and for this, take a small bowl, place all of its ingredients in it, stir until combined, and then spread evenly on top of meatloaf.

When the grill has preheated, open the lid, place loaf pan on the grill grate, shut the grill and smoke for 1 hour and 15 minutes until the internal temperature reaches 165 degrees F.

Serve straight away.

Nutrition: Calories: 186.5 Cal Fat: 7.2 g Carbs: 7.7 g Protein: 21.6 g Fiber: 0.4 g

Fish and Other Seafood Recipes

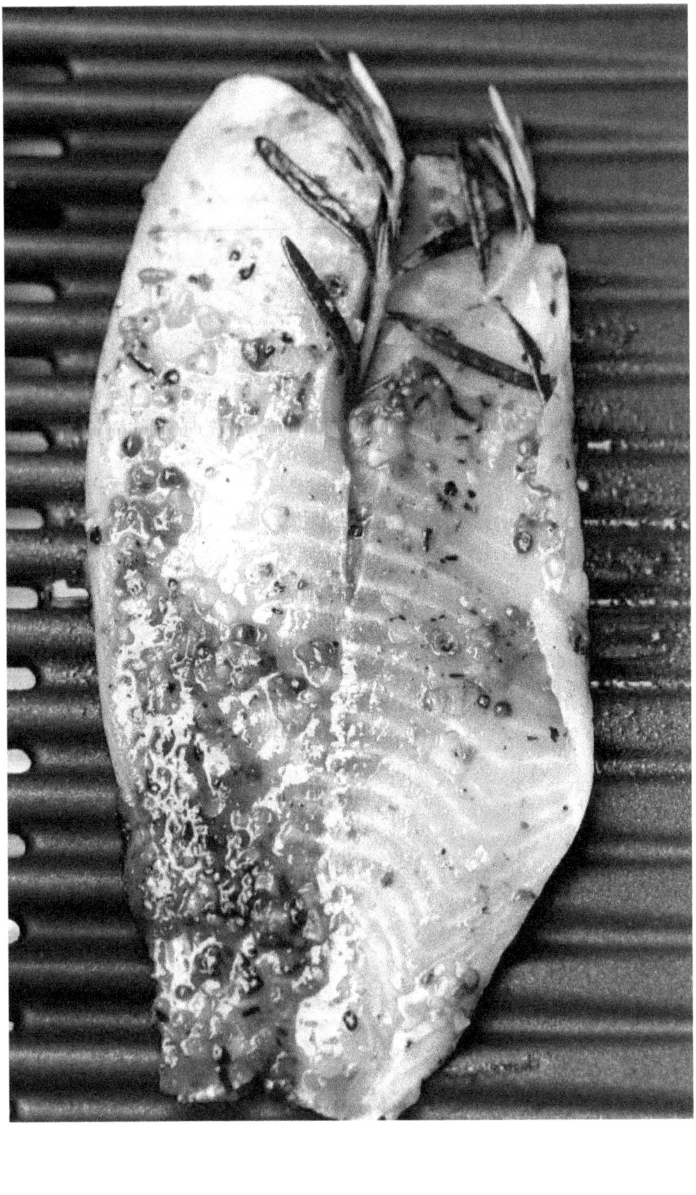

Grilled Lobster Tail

Preparation Time: 10 minutes
Cooking Time: 15 minutes
Servings: 4
Smoke Temperature: 450°F and 140°F
Ingredients:
2 (8 ounces each) lobster tails
1/4 tsp. old bay seasoning
½ tsp. oregano
1 tsp. paprika
Juice from one lemon
1/4 tsp. Himalayan salt
1/4 tsp. freshly ground black pepper
1/4 tsp. onion powder
2 tbsp. freshly chopped parsley
¼ cup melted butter
Directions:
Slice the tail in the middle with a kitchen shear. Pull the shell apart slightly and run your hand through the meat to separate the meat partially, keeping it attached to the base of the tail partially.
Combine the old bay seasoning, paprika, oregano, salt, pepper and onion powder in a mixing bowl.
Drizzle lobster tail with lemon juice and season generously with the seasoning mixture.
Preheat your wood pellet smoker to 450°F, using apple wood pellets.
Place the lobster tail directly on the grill grate, meat side down.
Cook for about 15 minutes or until the internal temperature of the tails reaches 140°F.
Take the tails off the grill and let them rest for a few minutes to cool.
Drizzle melted butter over the tails.
Serve and garnish with fresh chopped parsley.

Nutrition: *Calories 146 Total Fat 11.7g Saturated Fat 7.3g Cholesterol 56mg Sodium 295mg Total Carbohydrate 2.1g Dietary Fiber 0.8g Total Sugars 0.5g Protein 9.3g Vitamin D 8mcg Calcium 15mg Iron 0mg Potassium 53mg*

Halibut

Preparation Time: 10 minutes
Cooking Time: 30 minutes
Servings: 4
Smoke Temperature: 275°F and 135°F
Ingredients:
1 pound fresh halibut filet (cut into 4 equal sizes)
1 tbsp. fresh lemon juice
2 garlic cloves (minced)
2 tsp. soy sauce
½ tsp. ground black pepper
½ tsp. onion powder
2 tbsp. honey
½ tsp. oregano
1 tsp. dried basil
2 tbsp. butter (melted)
Maple syrup for serving
Directions:
In a mixing bowl, combine the lemon juice, honey, soy sauce, onion powder, oregano, dried basil, pepper and garlic.
Brush the halibut filets generously with the filet the mixture.
Wrap the filets with aluminum foil and refrigerate for 4 hours.
Remove the filets from the refrigerator and let them sit for about 2 hours, or until they are at room temperature.
Activate your wood pellet grill on smoke, leaving the lid opened for 5 minutes or until fire starts.
Heat your grill to 275°F for 15 minutes after closing the lid, using fruit wood pellets.
Place the halibut filets directly on the grill grate and smoke for 30 minutes or until the internal temperature of the fish reaches 135°F.
Remove the filets from the grill and let them rest for 10 minutes.
Serve and top with maple syrup to taste
Nutrition: *Calories 180 Total Fat 6.3g Saturated Fat 3.7g Cholesterol 35mg Sodium 247mg Total Carbohydrate 10g Dietary Fiber 0.3g Total Sugars 8.9g Protein 20.6g Vitamin D 4mcg Calcium 11mg Iron 0mg Potassium 34mg*

Grilled Salmon

Preparation Time: 10 minutes
Cooking Time: 30 minutes
Servings: 6
Smoke Temperature: 350°F
Ingredients:
2 pounds salmon (cut into fillets)
1/2 cup low sodium soy sauce
2 garlic cloves (grated)
4 tbsp. olive oil
2 tbsp. honey
1 tsp. ground black pepper
½ tsp. smoked paprika
½ tsp. Italian seasoning
Garnish:
2 tbsp. chopped green onion
Directions:
In a huge bowl, mix the honey, pepper, paprika, Italian seasoning, garlic, soy sauce and olive oil.
Add the salmon fillets and toss to combine. Cover the bowl and refrigerate for 1 hour.
Remove the fillets from the marinade and let it sit for about 2 hours, or until it is at room temperature.
Start the wood pellet on smoke, leaving the lid opened for 5 minutes, or until fire starts.
Close the lid and preheat grill to 350°F for 15 minutes.
Grease the grill grate with oil and arrange the fillets on the grill grate, skin side up. Close the grill lid and cook for 4 minutes.
Flip the fillets and cook for additional 25 minutes or until the fish is flaky.
Remove the fillets from heat and let it sit for a few minutes.
Serve warm and garnish with chopped green onion.
Nutrition: *Calories 317 Total Fat 18.8g Saturated Fat 2.7g Cholesterol 67mg Sodium 776mg Total Carbohydrate 8.3g Dietary Fiber 0.4g Total Sugars 6.2g Protein 30.6g Calcium 61mg Iron 2mg Potassium 635mg*

BBQ Shrimp

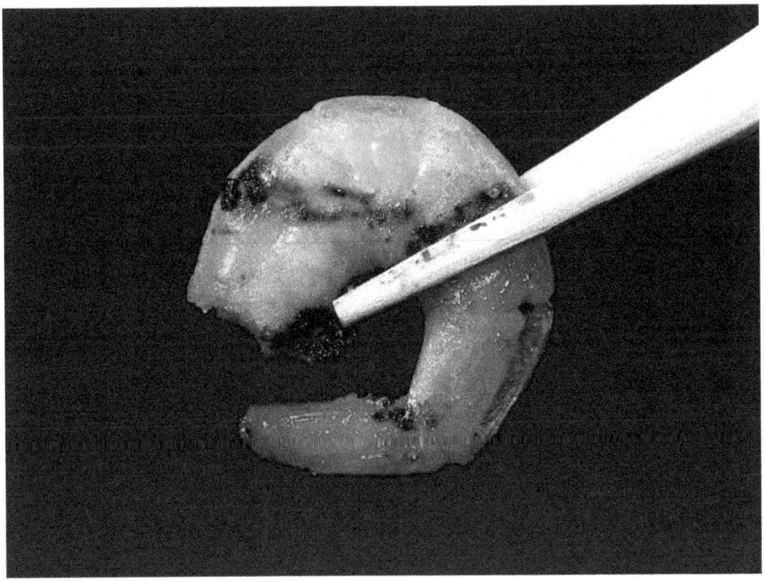

Preparation Time: 20 minutes
Cooking Time: 8 minutes
Servings: 6
Smoke Temperature: **450**°F
Ingredients:
2 pound raw shrimp (peeled and deveined)
¼ cup extra virgin olive oil
½ tsp. paprika
½ tsp. red pepper flakes
2 garlic cloves (minced)
1 tsp. cumin
1 lemon (juiced)
1 tsp. kosher salt
1 tbsp. chili paste
Bamboo or wooden skewers (soaked for 30 minutes, at least)
Directions:
In a large mixing bowl, combine the pepper flakes, cumin, lemon, salt, chili, paprika, garlic and olive oil. Add the shrimp and toss to combine.

Transfer the shrimp and marinade into a zip-lock bag and refrigerate for 4 hours.
Take the shrimp off the marinade and allow it to rest until it is a room temperature.
Start your grill on smoke, leaving the lid opened for 5 minutes, or until fire starts. Use hickory wood pellet.
Cover the lid and l allow the grill to heat to high for 15 minutes.
Thread shrimps onto skewers and arrange the skewers on the grill grate.
Smoke shrimps for 8 minutes, 4 minutes per side.
Serve and enjoy.
Nutrition: *Calories 267 Total Fat 11.6g Saturated Fat 2g Cholesterol 319mg Sodium 788mg Total Carbohydrate 4.9g Dietary Fiber 0.4g Total Sugars 1g Protein 34.9g Calcium 149mg Iron 1mg Potassium 287mg*

Grilled Tuna

Preparation Time: 5 minutes
Cooking Time: 4 minutes
Servings: 4
Smoke Temperature: 450°F
Ingredients:
4 (6 ounce each) tuna steaks (1 inch thick)
1 lemon (juiced)
1 clove garlic (minced)
1 tsp. chili
2 tbsp. extra virgin olive oil
1 cup white wine
3 tbsp. brown sugar
1 tsp. rosemary
Directions:
In a large mixing bowl, combine the chili, lemon, white wine, sugar, rosemary, olive oil and garlic. Add the tuna steaks and toss to combine.
Transfer the tuna and marinade to a Ziplock bag. Refrigerate for 3 hours.
Remove the tuna steaks from the marinade and let them rest for about 1 hour, or until the steaks are at room temperature.
Start your grill on smoke, leaving the lid opened for 5 minutes, or until fire starts. Use hickory or mesquite wood pellet.
Close the grill lid and let the grill heat on HIGH for 15 minutes.
Grease the grill grate with oil and place the tuna on the grill grate. Grill tuna steaks for 4 minutes, 2 minutes per side.
Remove the tuna from the grill and let them rest for a few minutes.
Serve and enjoy.

Nutrition: Calories 455 Total Fat 17.8g Saturated Fat 3.8g Cholesterol 84mg Sodium 97mg Total Carbohydrate 10.2g Dietary Fiber 0.6g Total Sugars 7.4g Protein 51.2g Calcium 37mg Iron 3mg Potassium 648mg

Oyster in Shell

Preparation Time: 25 minutes
Cooking Time: 8 minutes
Servings: 4
Smoke Temperature: **450**°F
Ingredients:
12 medium oysters
1 tsp. oregano
1 lemon (juiced)
1 tsp. freshly ground black pepper
6 tbsp. unsalted butter (melted)
1 tsp. salt or more to taste
2 garlic cloves (minced)
Garnish:
2 ½ tbsp. grated parmesan cheese
2 tbsp. freshly chopped parsley
Directions:
Start by scrubbing the outside of the shell with a scrub brush under cold running water to remove dirt.
Hold an oyster in a towel, flat side up. Insert an oyster knife in the hinge of the oyster.
Twist the knife with pressure to pop open the oyster. Run the knife along the oyster hinge to open the shell completely. Discard the top shell.
Gently run the knife under the oyster to loosen the oyster foot from the bottom shell.
Repeat step 2 and 3 for the remaining oysters.
Combine melted butter, lemon, pepper, salt, garlic and oregano in a mixing bowl.
Pour ½ to 1 tsp. of the butter mixture on each oyster.
Start your wood pellet grill on smoke, leaving the lid opened for 5 minutes, or until fire starts.
Close the lid and let the grill heat to high with lid closed for 15 minutes.
Gently arrange the oysters onto the grill grate.
Grill oyster for 6 to 8 minutes or until the oyster juice is bubbling and the oyster is plump.

Remove oysters from heat. Serve and top with grated parmesan and chopped parsley.

Nutrition: *Calories 200 Total Fat 19.2g Saturated Fat 11.9g Cholesterol 66mg Sodium 788mg Total Carbohydrate 3.9g Dietary Fiber 0.8g Total Sugars 0.7g Protein 4.6g Vitamin D 12mcg Calcium 93mg Iron 2mg Potassium 120mg*

Grilled King Crab Legs

Preparation Time: 10 minutes
Cooking Time: 25 minutes
Servings: 4
Smoke Temperature: 225°F
Ingredients:
4 pounds king crab legs (split)
4 tbsp. lemon juice
2 tbsp. garlic powder
1 cup butter (melted)
2 tsp. brown sugar
2 tsp. paprika
2 tsp. ground black pepper or more to taste
Directions:
In a mixing bowl, combine the lemon juice, butter, sugar, garlic, paprika and pepper.
Arrange the split crab on a baking sheet, split side up.
Drizzle ¾ of the butter mixture over the crab legs.
Configure your pellet grill for indirect cooking and preheat it to 225°F, using mesquite wood pellets.
Arrange the crab legs onto the grill grate, shell side down.
Cover the grill and cook 25 minutes.
Remove the crab legs from the grill.
Serve and top with the remaining butter mixture.

Nutrition: Calories 894 Total Fat 53.2g 68% Saturated Fat 29.3g 147% Cholesterol 374mg 125% Sodium 5189mg 226% Total Carbohydrate 6.1g Dietary Fiber 1.2g Total Sugars 3g Protein 88.6g Vitamin D 32mcg Calcium 301mg Iron 4mg Potassium 119mg

Cajun Smoked Catfish

Preparation Time: 15 minutes
Cooking Time: 2 hours
Servings: 4
Smoke Temperature: 200°F
Ingredients:
4 catfish fillets (5 ounces each)
½ cup Cajun seasoning
1 tsp. ground black pepper
1 tbsp. smoked paprika
1 /4 tsp. cayenne pepper
1 tsp. hot sauce
1 tsp. granulated garlic
1 tsp. onion powder
1 tsp. thyme
1 tsp. salt or more to taste
2 tbsp. chopped fresh parsley
Directions:
Pour water into the bottom of a square or rectangular dish. Add 4 tbsp. salt. Arrange the catfish fillets into the dish. Cover the dish and refrigerate for 3 to 4 hours.
Meanwhile, combine the paprika, cayenne, hot sauce, onion, salt, thyme, garlic, pepper and Cajun seasoning in a mixing bowl.
Remove the fish from the dish and let it sit for a few minutes, or until it is at room temperature. Pat the fish fillets dry with a paper towel.
Rub the seasoning mixture over each fillet generously.
Start your grill on smoke, leaving the lid opened for 5 minutes, or until fire starts.
Cover the lid and allow the grill to heat to 200°F, using mesquite hardwood pellets.
Arrange the fish fillets onto the grill grate and close the grill. Cook for about 2 hours, or until the fish is flaky.
Remove the fillets from the grill and let the fillets rest for a few minutes to cool.
Serve and garnish with chopped fresh parsley.

Nutrition: *Calories 204 Total Fat 11.1g Saturated Fat 2g Cholesterol 67mg Sodium 991mg Total Carbohydrate 2.7g Dietary Fiber 1.1g Total Sugars 0.6g Protein 22.9g Calcium 29mg Iron 3mg Potassium 532mg*

Vegan and Sides Recipes

Roasted Cauliflower

Preparation Time: 15min
Cooking Time: 10min
Servings: 4 to 6
Smoke Temperature: **450**°F and 180°F
Ingredients:
1 Cauliflower head, cut into florets
1 tbsp. Oil
1 cup grated Parmesan
2 Garlic cloves, cursed
½ Tsp. Black pepper
½ tsp. of Salt
¼ tsp. of Paprika
Directions:
Let the grill heat to 180F with closed lid.
Place the cauliflower florets on the grill. Smoke 1 hour. In the meantime combine the remaining ingredients but not the cheese. Once done remove the florets.
Increase the heat to 450F. Once heated brush the florets with the mixture. Place on a cooking tray and on the grill. Roast for 10 min.
Sprinkle with cheese and let it sit on the grill with closed lid until melted.
Serve as it is or as a side dish. Enjoy!

Nutrition: *Calories: 45 Protein: 7g Carbs: 7g Fat: 2g*

Roasted Asparagus

Preparation Time: 5 minutes
Cooking Time: 30 minutes
Servings: 4 to 6
Smoke Temperature: 350°F
Ingredients:
1 bunch of Asparagus
Salmon seasoning as needed
2 tbsp. Oil, or as needed
Directions:
Season the asparagus with salmon seasoning and drizzle with oil. Make sure to coat well.
Let the grill heat to 350F with closed lid.
Grill the asparagus for 30 minutes.
Serve and enjoy!
Nutrition: Calories: 70g Protein: 4g Carbs: 7g Fat: 4g

Grilled Mixed Veggies

Preparation Time: 15 minutes
Cooking Time: 20 minutes
Servings: 4 to 6
Smoke Temperature: 450°F
Ingredients:
1 Tomato, Large
1 Squash
1 Zucchini
1 Onion, red
1 Potato, Sweet
Black pepper and Salt to taste
Oil
Directions:
Let the grill heat with closed lit to high.
Slice the veggies into slices (1/4 inch).
Brush each slice with oil. Season with black pepper and salt.
First grill the squash; zucchini, onion and sweet potato for 20min. turn them halfway.
Add the tomato slices 5 minutes before the cooking is done.
Serve them with your main dish and enjoy!
Nutrition: Calories: 105 Protein: 5g Carbs: 23g Fat: 8g

Grilled Corn

Preparation Time: 15 minutes
Cooking Time: 25 minutes
Servings: 6
Smoke Temperature: **450**°F
Ingredients:
6 fresh ears corn
Salt
Black pepper
Olive oil
Vegetable seasoning
Butter for serving
Directions:
Let the grill heat to high with closed lid.
Peel the husks. Remove the corn's silk. Rub with black pepper, salt, vegetable seasoning, and oil.
Close the husks and grill for 25 minutes. Turn them occasionally.
Serve topped with butter and enjoy!

Nutrition: Calories: 70 Protein: 3g Carbs: 18g Fat: 2g

Thyme - Rosemary Mash Potatoes

Preparation Time: 20 minutes
Cooking Time: 1 hour
Servings: 6
Smoke Temperature: **350**°F
Ingredients:
4 ½ lbs. Potatoes, russet
Salt
1 pint of Heavy cream
3 Thyme sprigs + 2 tbsp. for garnish
2 Rosemary sprigs
6 - 7 Sage leaves
6 - 7 Black peppercorns
Black pepper to taste

2 stick Butter, softened
2 Garlic cloves, chopped

Directions:

Let the grill heat to 350F with closed lid.

Peel the russet potatoes. Cut into small pieces and place them in a baking dish. Fill it with water (1 ½ cups). Place on the grill and cook with closed lid for about 1 hour.

In the meantime in a saucepan combine the garlic, peppercorns, herbs, and cream. Place on the grate and cook covered for about 15 minutes. Once done, strain to remove the garlic and herbs. Keep warm.

Drain the potatoes and place them in a stockpot. Rice them with a fork and pour 2/3 of the mixture. Add 1 stick softened butter and salt. Add more cream to get the desired consistency.

Serve right away.

Nutrition: Calories: 180 Protein: 4g Carbs: 28g Fat: 10g

Grilled Broccoli

Preparation Time: 15 minutes
Cooking Time: 10 minutes
Servings: 4 to 6
Smoke Temperature: 450°F
Ingredients:
4 bunches of Broccoli
4 tbsp. Olive oil
Black pepper and salt to taste
½ Lemon, the juice
½ Lemon cut into wedges
Directions:
Let the grill heat to High with closed lid.
In a bowl add the broccoli and drizzle with oil. Coat well. Season with salt.
Grill for 5 minutes and then flip. Cook for 3 minutes more.
Once done transfer on a plate. Squeeze lemon on top and serve with lemon wedges. Enjoy!

Nutrition: *Calories: 35g Protein: 2.5g Carbs: 5g Fat: 1g*

Smoked Coleslaw

Preparation Time: 15 minutes
Cooking Time: 25 minutes
Servings: 8 to 12
Smoke Temperature: 180°F
Ingredients:
1 shredded Purple Cabbage
1 shredded Green Cabbage
2 Scallions, sliced
1 cup Carrots, shredded
1 tbsp. of Celery Seed
1/8 cup of White vinegar
1 ½ cups Mayo
Black pepper and salt to taste
Directions:
Let the grill heat to 180F with closed lid.
On a tray spread the carrots and cabbage. Place the tray on the grate and smoke for about 25 minutes.
Transfer in the fridge to cool.
In the meantime make the dressing. In a bowl combine the ingredients. Mix well.
Transfer the veggies in a bowl. Drizzle with the sauce and toss
Serve sprinkled with scallions. You can serve it as a side dish or as a salad. Enjoy!

Nutrition: Calories: 35g Protein: 1g Carbs: 5g Fat: 5g

The Best Potato Roast

Preparation Time: 15 minutes
Cooking Time: 35 minutes
Servings: 6
Smoke Temperature: 450°F
Ingredients:
4 Potatoes, large (scrubbed)
2 tbsp. Vegetable oil
1 ½ cups gravy (beef or chicken)
Rib seasoning to taste
1 ½ cups Cheddar cheese
Black pepper and salt to taste
2 tbsp. sliced Scallions
Directions:
Let the grill heat to high with closed lid.
Slice each potato into wedges or fries. Transfer into a bowl and drizzle with oil. Season with Rib seasoning.
Spread the wedges/fries on a baking sheet (rimmed). Roast for about 20 minutes. Turn the wedges/fries and cook for 15 minutes more.
In the meantime in a saucepan warm the chicken/beef gravy. Cut the cheese into small cubes.
Once done cooking place the potatoes on a plate or into a bowl. Distribute the cut cheese and pour hot gravy on top.
Serve garnished with scallion. Season with pepper. Enjoy!

Nutrition: *Calories: 220 Protein: 3g Carbs: 38g Fat: 15g*

Sauces

Bourbon Barbecue Sauce

Preparation Time: 5 minutes
Cooking Time: 40 minutes
Servings: 8 to 12
Ingredients:
½ onion (minced)
¾ cup bourbon whiskey
4 cloves garlic (minced)
½ teaspoon black pepper (ground)
2 cups ketchup

⅓ Cup cider vinegar
½ tablespoon salt
¼ cup tomato paste
½ cup packed brown sugar
¼ cup Worcestershire sauce
⅓ Teaspoons hot pepper sauce (or add as you see fit)

Directions:

Set your wood pellet smoker grill for indirect cooking.

Let the grill heat at 350 degrees Fahrenheit for 15 minutes, with the lid closed.

Grab a large skillet, and add your garlic, whiskey, and onion. Let it all simmer for 20 minutes on your smoker grill. You're waiting for the onions to get translucent.

Toss in the salt, ground black pepper, tomato paste, ketchup, Worcestershire sauce, vinegar, brown sugar, and hot pepper sauce. Mix it all up.

Bring it all to a boil, then drop the heat to 225 degrees Fahrenheit and then let it simmer for 20 minutes more.

If you like your sauce smooth, then use a strainer to extract it from the onions and stuff.

Enjoy this sauce with your barbecue meals!

Best pellets: hickory

Nutrition: Calories: 30 Protein: 15g Carbs: 5g

Texas Style Coffee Mop Sauce

Preparation Time: 5 minutes
Cooking Time: 25 minutes
Servings: 8 to 12
Ingredients:
1 tablespoon sugar
1 cup Catsup
¼ cup butter
½ cup Worcestershire sauce
1 cup dark or strong coffee
1 tablespoon black pepper (fresh, coarse, ground)
1 tablespoon kosher salt
Directions:
Mix all your ingredients in a pot large enough to allow you to work without it spilling over
Set up your smoker grill for direct cooking
Preheat your smoker grill to 350 degrees Fahrenheit for 15 minutes, with the lid closed.
Now simmer your ingredients on your smoker grill for 20 minutes. Allow it to thicken. Enjoy!
Nutrition: Calories: 35 Protein: 18g Carbs: 7g

Beer Mopping Sauce

Preparation Time: 5 minutes
Cooking Time: 20 minutes
Servings: 8 to 12
Ingredients:
12 ounces of beer
½ cup water
½ cup cider vinegar
½ cup canola or corn oil
½ onion (medium, chopped)
2 garlic cloves (minced)
1 tablespoon Worcestershire sauce
1 tablespoon brisket seasoning
Directions:
Whisk your ingredients all together in a saucepan.
Set up the grill for direct cooking
Let the grill heat at 350 degrees Fahrenheit for 15 minutes, with the lid closed.
Let your ingredients simmer on the grates, till they come to a boil, then lower the heat.
Let it get nice and thick, and then take it off the grill, and let it cool
Best pellets: hickory

Nutrition: Calories: 40 Protein: 10g Carbs: 4g

Carolina Mopping Sauce

Preparation Time: 5 minutes
Cooking Time: 5 minutes
Servings: 8 to 12
Ingredients:
1 cup cider vinegar
1 tablespoon hot sauce
1 tablespoon red pepper flakes
1 cup distilled white
1 teaspoon onion powder
1 teaspoon garlic powder
2 tablespoons brown sugar (packed)
1 teaspoon dry mustard
½ teaspoon salt
¼ teaspoon black pepper (ground)
Directions:
Simply mix all your ingredients together, and then store in an air-tight fridge for a month.
If you need more heat, just add some more red pepper flakes.
Nutrition: Calories: 26 Protein: 17g Carbs: 6g

Pulled Pork Mop Recipe

Preparation Time: 5 minutes
Cooking Time: 5 minutes
Servings: 8 to 12
Ingredients:
16 ounces cider vinegar
16 ounces vegetable oil
32 ounces water
1 cup ultra-dry rub
2 tablespoons Worcestershire sauce
2 tablespoons soy sauce
Directions:
Simply whisk all the ingredients together, after dissolving your dry rub with some hot water.
Nutrition: Calories: 40 Protein: 19g Carbs: 8g

Apple Butter and Fireball BBQ Sauce

Preparation Time: 10 minutes
Cooking Time: 60 minutes
Servings: 3
Ingredients:
1 tablespoon olive oil
½ yellow onion, diced
3 garlic cloves, minced
1 ½ cups apple butter
½ cup cinnamon whiskey, such as Fireball
½ cup ketchup
1/3 cup apple cider vinegar
½ cup brown sugar, packed
2 tablespoons Worcestershire sauce
1 teaspoon cayenne pepper flakes
1 teaspoon ground mustard
1 teaspoon ground black pepper
1 teaspoon salt
Directions:
Coat the bottom of a saucepan with the oil.
Add the garlic and onion and place on the stove over medium heat, sautéing the onions until they become translucent.
Pour the cinnamon whiskey into the saucepan with the tender vegetables and stir until well combined.
Bring the mixture to a boil before reducing the heat and simmering for 10 minutes, while stirring frequently.
While the mixture is simmering, combine the ketchup, apple butter, Worcestershire sauce, vinegar, mustard, brown sugar, salt, black pepper, and cayenne pepper in a mixing bowl.
Combine the mixture from Step 3 into the mixture from Step 2. Turn the heat up and bring the mixture back to a boil, while stirring regularly. Once it boils, reduce the heat again and let it simmer for 25 to 30 minutes.
Take the saucepan off the heat and let it cool down. Use immediately or pour into mason jars and store in the fridge until ready to use.

Nutrition: Calories: 50 Protein: 26g Carbs: 8g

Spicy and Sweet Jalapeno BBQ Sauce

Preparation Time: 10 minutes
Cooking Time: 30 minutes
Servings: 2
Ingredients:
½ cup butter, unsalted
½ cup brown sugar, packed
1 whole jalapeno, grilled for about 2 minutes
15 ounces tomato sauce, canned
½ cup apple cider vinegar
1 tablespoon Worcestershire sauce
1 tablespoon onion powder
1 tablespoon garlic powder
1 teaspoon salt
1 teaspoon ground mustard
1 teaspoon cumin
½ teaspoon ground cayenne pepper
Directions:
Place the butter in a saucepan. Set the pan on the stove over medium heat and melt the butter.
Stir in the brown sugar, bring to a boil, and boil for about 5 minutes.
Place the grilled jalapeno pepper into a blender. Add the tomato sauce and blend until there are no chunks left.
Transfer the tomato mixture into the butter mixture.
Add the Worcestershire sauce, onion powder, vinegar, ground mustard, salt, cayenne pepper, cumin, and garlic powder. Stir until well combined.
Let the mixture simmer for 30 minutes, making sure to stir the mixture frequently.
Remove the sauce from the heat and let it cool down a bit.
Use the sauce immediately or transfer to a mason jar. Store unused BBQ sauce in the fridge for up to 7 to 10 days.

Nutrition: Calories: 55 Protein: 20g Carbs: 6g

Honey-BB BBQ Sauce

Preparation Time: 10 minutes
Cooking Time: 35minutes
Servings: 3
Ingredients:
1 tablespoon dark brown sugar, packed
2 tablespoons chili powder
1 tablespoon smoked paprika
1 tablespoon sage, dried
1 tablespoon yellow mustard, ground
1 teaspoon kosher salt
½ teaspoon cayenne powder
1 small to medium-sized yellow onion, chopped roughly
8 ounces smoked bacon, chopped roughly
1 large shot glass bourbon
4 garlic cloves, chopped roughly
½ cup espresso, strongly brewed
½ cup coffee, strongly brewed
1 cup ketchup
2 tablespoon honey
1 tablespoon soy sauce
Directions:
Cook the bacon in a skillet over medium heat for about 8 to 10 minutes. Stir in the garlic and onion and continue to cook for an additional 8 to 10 minutes.
Stir the brown sugar, chili powder, paprika, sage, salt, and cayenne powder into the bacon mixture until well mixed.
Add the bourbon to deglaze the pan. Remove the skillet from the heat and transfer to a blender or food processor.
Pour the espresso, coffee, honey, soy sauce, and ketchup into the food processor with the bacon mixture. Blend the mixture until it is completely smooth.
Transfer the BBQ sauce into a mason jar and close securely. Keep the sauce inside the fridge until its ready to be used.

Nutrition: Calories: 45 Protein: 20g Carbs: 4g

Hawaiian-Inspired BBQ Sauce

Preparation Time: 10 minutes
Cooking Time: 30 minutes
Servings: 3
Ingredients:
1 ½ tablespoons ginger, grated finely
3 garlic cloves, minced
1 cup ketchup, all-natural
¼ cup dark brown sugar, packed
½ tablespoon dry mustard
½ cup soy sauce, low-sodium
½ teaspoon chili powder
¼ teaspoon white pepper
¼ cup orange juice, freshly squeezed
8 ounces crushed pineapple
Directions:
Place all the ingredients in a saucepan. Put the saucepan over the stove and let the ingredients boil.
Once boiling, reduce heat to a simmer.
Let the mixture simmer for about 35 to 40 minutes. The sauce should reduce by half. Once this occurs, take the saucepan off the heat.
Move the sauce to a mason jar if you do not intend to use it immediately. Store unused sauce in the fridge for up to 7 days.

Nutrition: Calories: 45 Protein: 20g Carbs: 7g

Root Beer BBQ Sauce

Preparation Time: 15 minutes
Cooking Time: 2 hours
Servings: 3
Ingredients:
2 tablespoons oil, vegetable or canola
1 small onion, diced
1 ½ cups root beer
¼ cup brown sugar, packed
¼ cup apple cider vinegar
½ teaspoon cumin
15 ounces diced tomatoes, canned
½ to 1 teaspoon cayenne pepper
Directions:
Place the oil in a saucepan. Put the saucepan over the stove and let it heat.
Once warm, add the onions and sauté until they become translucent.
Stir in the rest of the ingredients and bring the mixture to a boil while stirring frequently.
Once the mixture starts to boil, reduce the heat and let it simmer for about 40 minutes.
Take the saucepan off the heat and let it cool a little before blending the sauce in a blender until smooth.
Pour the sauce back into the saucepan and simmer for an hour.
Remove the sauce from heat and let it cool completely.
Transfer the sauce into a pint-sized Mason jar and store in the fridge.

Nutrition: Calories: 28 Protein: 14g Carbs: 6g

Other Tips and Tricks

Even if you are a novice who lacks enough experience when it comes to BBQ, we are here to share some of the best tips and tricks with you. After you have gone through this part of the book, you will be in a better place to make much better meals and become a pro at using BBQ.

Don't Lose Patience

It is very important to be patient when you are cooking. Do not be in a rush when you are barbecuing as the authentic taste only comes when you allow the meat to be cooked slowly and thoroughly.

Placing the Meat

When you are looking for a barbecue, it is very important to learn the right placement of meat. If you put the meat on the grill immediately on heating the flame, it is likely to be scorched on the outside and the sides won't cook well. You can do this for steaks but anything else; put them on the grill after the flames have died down. That will produce even cooking results.

The Pre-Heat

Do not take pre-heat lightly. Based on the chosen recipe, some of the sausages and other meat products may need to be cooked a little before transferring them to the grill. Alternately, after barbecuing them, they have to be placed on the baking tray as well. So, pay heed to these little factors thoroughly and meticulously.

Maintaining the Temperature Guidelines

Barbecue is all about getting the temperature right. When the flame is on, you may find it hard to judge how hot or cold the flame is. Here is a rough idea of the approximation of the kind of heat which is present.

You can place your hand almost 12 cm above the grill and then use this time (how long you can keep your hand at that length) as a measurement to indicate the heat level.

•2 seconds: very high hat
•4 seconds: medium heat
•6 seconds: low heat

Also, you can use the half and half technique which means that all the coals should be moved to one side. This would ensure that your grill would have two portions- one would be extremely hot and the other would have no access to the direct heat.
So, be mindful of these points and regulate the temperature in the right manner.

Use Aluminum Foil for Easy Cleaning

Cleaning might be a difficult job to do especially after the guests are gone and your tummy is full. This is why you can line the insides with a few aluminum foils before putting the briquettes in. So, when you are done barbecuing and things have cooled up a little, simply take off the foil and you are good to go.
Immerse the wood chips under the water before you start to cook
If you want to get the most amazing Smokey flavor and you are on the lookout to increase the overall smoke when you grill, a golden tip to use is to soak the wood chips in water at least an hour before you put them in the grill. Better still, if you can soak them overnight, it might do wonders. You should then wrap them in an aluminum foil like a burrito and then put them on the grill.
This is so done because the water content inside it helps in the production of thicker smoke and thereby enhances the overall flavor.

Using the Right Tools

When you are looking to have a barbecue feast, there is absolutely no way you can be reckless with your choices. This is why regardless of the kind of expense it may entail; we want you to use the easy blend of tools when cooking. The kind of tongs you are using for flipping over the meat or any other product and anything else should be top-notch. Do not compromise with the tools and equipment as it all plays a role when it comes to the true taste of barbecue.

Marinating Is the Key

Like we have told, when it comes to barbecue; 'Authentic' is the watchword here. So, if a recipe says to add marinade, make sure you do that. Brushing the meat or even the fish with marinade every 10 to 15 minutes while it is being cooked might be a great way to get the best result. Doing this adds moisture and also traps the flavor of the smoke. This enhances the flavor a great deal.

Use the Veggies

Barbecue and non-veg products are always used in sync. Barbecue is a great way to smoke the vegetables and adds a characteristic flavor to them as well. Slice your veggies and then grill them headlong. You do not need any oil. When they have been thoroughly cooked, you can sprinkle olive oil and vinegar and then the taste is going to take your food buds on a real ride. Try them out today!

Conclusion

Thank you for making it to the end. Grilling summer season never gets to an end, especially if you call yourself a pit-master down your heart. And whether you love grilling with your friends or family in your backyard or even if you want to grill by yourself; you would want an innovative and creative grilling technique. Yet, it is challenging sometimes and extremely tough to use a gas or wood grill because of the huge mess and the cleaning process that will exhaust your and prevent you from enjoying grilling the way you want. And other times, even using your favorite grill can't give you the results you want neither gives you the flavors you are looking for. So have you ever wondered about what you can do to resolve this and make grilling one of the memorable experiences you will ever get?
Just imagine finding the grill that combines the versatility, the convenience and the ease of using a gas grill and the flavor of hardwood and smoke into your grilled ingredients? Does it sound that your dream will come true? If yes, pellet grill will be your magical and at the same time your real grill that combines the advantages of gas grill and hardwood barbecue to offer you an incredible taste only with the use of your favorite type of pellets like apple or oak pellets. Using pellet smoker or grills will not only offer you a great versatility, but also a great pack of flavor you have never imagined you would get.

Does it sound impossible for you? Well, the unmatched flavor pellet grills offer are so real and you will be surprised at how easy pellet grills are simple to use, to clean and to cook a wide variety of food ingredients. Pellet smoker and grills can play the role of ovens, grills and you will be amazed at how practical this type of pellet grills is. This cookbook will help you properly learn how to use the revolutionary and creative cooking device known as pellet grills by offering you various and useful tips. Pellet grills are only fueled by pellets which will make your experience healthier and safer. You can infuse the flavor you want through the type of pellets you want. You will be surprised that the Hardwood pellet cooker looks exactly like a classic smoker and that the Pellet grill perfectly fits into outdoor areas and outdoor kitchens alike.

If you have guests you don't have to worry anymore because now you will be able to enjoy chit chats with them while you food is being grilled thanks to the Pellet grills. And thanks to this easy-to follow cookbook, you will be able to cook a large array of recipes that you will enjoy.

Thank you for reading this book.

I am happy and proud to have been able to offer you this wood pellet recipe cookbook and I am extremely happy that I have introduced you to the world of wood pellet grills and I am excited to hear your suggestions and how the cooking results will be. This cookbook would have never come to life without your help and support.

I hope that you will share this cookbook with your friends and dear ones. Please, feel free to share your thoughts with us and to help us create the healthy environment you want. Get ready to enjoy some of the most entertaining cooking experiences that you will ever be able to enjoy.

About The Author

The author of this book is a writer and an editor who delights in cooking. His passion for grilling has brought him to learn so much, particularly, about smoking meats and vegetables. He has worked with various companies in the outdoor-cooking industry, and was the official grill master during that time.

CPSIA information can be obtained
at www.ICGtesting.com
Printed in the USA
BVHW061412250221
601119BV00001B/134

9 781801 861052